Anne Hutchinson

Religious Leader

Colonial Leaders

Lord Baltimore *English Politician and Colonist*

Benjamin Banneker *American Mathematician and Astronomer*

William Bradford *Governor of Plymouth Colony*

Benjamin Franklin *American Statesman, Scientist, and Writer*

Anne Hutchinson *Religious Leader*

Cotton Mather *Author, Clergyman, and Scholar*

William Penn *Founder of Democracy*

John Smith *English Explorer and Colonist*

Miles Standish *Plymouth Colony Leader*

Peter Stuyvesant *Dutch Military Leader*

Revolutionary War Leaders

Benedict Arnold *Traitor to the Cause*

Nathan Hale *Revolutionary Hero*

Alexander Hamilton *First U.S. Secretary of the Treasury*

Patrick Henry *American Statesman and Speaker*

Thomas Jefferson *Author of the Declaration of Independence*

John Paul Jones *Father of the U.S. Navy*

Thomas Paine *Political Writer*

Paul Revere *American Patriot*

Betsy Ross *American Patriot*

George Washington *First U.S. President*

Anne Hutchinson

Religious Leader

Beth Clark

Arthur M. Schlesinger, jr.
Senior Consulting Editor

Chelsea House Publishers

Philadelphia

Produced by Robert Gerson Publisher's Services, Avondale, PA

CHELSEA HOUSE PUBLISHERS
Editor in Chief Stephen Reginald
Production Manager Pamela Loos
Director of Photography Judy L. Hasday
Art Director Sara Davis
Managing Editor James D. Gallagher

Staff for *ANNE HUTCHINSON*
Project Editor Anne Hill
Project Editor/Publishing Coordinator Jim McAvoy
Contributing Editor Amy Handy
Associate Art Director Takeshi Takahashi
Series Design Keith Trego

The Chelsea House World Wide Web address is http://www.chelseahouse.com

3 5 7 9 8 6 4 2

Library of Congress Cataloging-in-Publication Data

Clark, Beth, 1967–
Anne Hutchinson / by Beth Clark.
    p. cm.— (Colonial leaders)
Includes bibliographical references.
Summary: A biography of the Puritan woman who was banished from the
Massachusetts Bay Colony for disagreeing with the prevailing religious practices.
ISBN 0-7910-5342-3 (hc); 0-7910-5685-6 (pb)
1. Hutchinson, Anne Marbury, 1591–1643 Juvenile literature.   2. Puritans—
Massachusetts Biography Juvenile literature.   3. Massachusetts—History—
Colonial period, ca. 1600–1775 Juvenile literature. [1. Hutchinson, Anne
Marbury, 1591–1643.   2. Puritans.   3. Massachusetts—History—Colonial period,
ca. 1600–1775.   4. Freedom of religion—History.] I. Title.   II. Series.
F67.H92C58   1999
974.4'02'092—dc21
[B]   99–21553
                                                                CIP

Publisher's Note: In Colonial and Revolutionary War America, there were no standard rules for spelling, punctuation, capitalization, or grammar. Some of the quotations that appear in the Colonial Leaders and Revolutionary War Leaders series come from original documents and letters written during this time in history. Original quotations reflect writing inconsistencies of the period.

Contents

1 Mistress Hutchinson   7

2 Speaking Her Mind   21

3 The Troubles Begin   31

4 Mrs. Hutchinson on Trial   41

5 Faithful to the End   55

   Glossary   68

   Chronology   69

   Colonial Time Line   71

   Further Reading   73

   Index   74

Anne Hutchinson was born in the small English village of Alford, more than a hundred miles from the bustle of London. Her childhood hometown probably looked something like this one.

Mistress Hutchinson

On July 17, 1591, Reverend Francis Marbury and his wife, Bridget, became the proud parents of a baby girl who would grow up to change her world. This little girl named Anne was the second of their 13 children. The Marbury family lived in the small town of Alford, England, where Anne's father worked as a minister. Born during a time when many religious changes were taking place in England, Anne would see and be a part of even more changes throughout her life.

For years, everyone in England had been Catholic. Then, almost 100 years before Anne was born, King Henry VIII of England left the

Catholic Church. He wanted to divorce his wife, but the Catholic Church would not let its members get divorced. Because he was determined to end his marriage, he started a new church called the Church of England. He made himself the head of the church, and from that time until today, the king or queen of England has also been the ruler of the Church of England. When political rulers are also religious rulers, the government is called a **theocracy**.

The English people did not want their church to be exactly like the Catholic Church, but they could not agree on how much to change it. One group wanted more change than the others. They wanted a more relaxed and simple form of worship that would be much less formal than Catholic Church services. These people were known as the **Puritans** because they wanted a "pure" religion without the rules and ceremonies of Catholicism.

Several members of Anne's mother's family were Puritans, and her father, Reverend Marbury, was accused of being a Puritan. He did not

Like the other countries in Europe, England had
been Catholic until King Henry VIII broke away
from the Catholic Church in order to get a
divorce.

approve of the way the church selected ministers. Some men became preachers because their families knew political rulers or because they were wealthy. Reverend Marbury, on the other hand, had spent years going to school and earning his degree at Cambridge University. In fact, he spoke against untrained ministers so much that he was even thrown in jail and not allowed to preach for several years.

Because her father had always expressed his opinions, Anne Marbury grew up feeling free to speak her mind. She often heard him disagree with the rules of the Church of England. Many times her father's friends would gather at the Marbury home to discuss their views on religion and Anne would listen to them. During the time he was not allowed to preach, Reverend Marbury spent time farming his fields, writing, and teaching Anne about the Bible. He knew that Anne was a serious child and was much brighter than other girls her age. From a young age she wanted to learn about God and about how people worship God. Because her father was an educated man, he was able to give Anne a better education than most young English girls received and to encourage her to stay curious and always to keep learning.

Before long Reverend Marbury knew he needed to make enough money to support his family. He decided to preach again and to keep quiet about his feelings toward the Church of England. The Marbury family moved about 125 miles from the village of Alford to the city of London. Reverend Marbury worked at a church in London until his death in 1611.

Anne was 21 years old when her father died. Her interest in religion and worship continued. She wanted to become a minister, but women were not allowed to be ministers at that time. She began to wonder if any man would want to marry her if she ever did become a minister. Most young English women married much earlier than 21, so she began to think she might be single for the rest of her life.

Soon Anne fell in love with William Hutchinson. Anne and William had known each other in Alford, but were both living in London when he asked her to marry him. Their wedding took place on August 9, 1612. After they married, they moved back to Alford. Their first child was born the following year.

In villages such as Alford, outside of London, people felt more free to disagree with the Church of England. In several of the towns close to Alford, some women actually became preachers even though the Church of England did not approve of female ministers. Other ministers began to preach more and more about Puritan ideas. Mrs. Hutchinson had never lost her childhood desire to study and explore religious beliefs, and she was pleased to hear about a nearby minister who shared some of her opinions.

Reverend John Cotton was the most popular minister in England. He preached at St. Botolph's Church in the town of Boston, about

24 miles from Anne's home in Alford. Reverend Cotton was a young minister, full of energy and bold enough to preach the Puritan message. News about John Cotton spread quickly and soon the Hutchinsons were traveling to Boston to hear him preach each week.

One of the Church of England's ideas that most bothered Anne Hutchinson was called the **Covenant of Works**. Under the Covenant of Works, church leaders made rules for people and believed that the truly religious people were the ones who obeyed the rules. They believed that the only way for people to get to heaven was to keep from sinning and to do many good deeds.

This Covenant of Works also bothered John Cotton. He believed that all people were sinners and that a person could not do enough good works to earn God's love. He believed that people were saved and sent to heaven by complete faith in God, and not by holy actions. This belief became known as the **Covenant of Grace**.

Under the Covenant of Works, the Church was able to judge people because of its rules. Under the Covenant of Grace, people judged themselves because of God's love.

The more Anne Hutchinson thought and learned about the Covenant of Grace, the more she believed in it. But the more she and others believed in it, the more the Church of England tried to stop it. They wanted people to live by the Covenant of Works, and began to arrest preachers who taught about the Covenant of Grace. A new king, Charles I, also began to punish Puritan ministers by asking them to stop preaching or by demanding that they preach the Covenant of Works. He also arrested many Puritan ministers and put them in prison. In 1622 John Cotton was arrested for his preaching, but did not go to jail. Just being arrested was enough to make him think about leaving England and moving to a place where he could preach what he truly believed.

One October day in 1632 John Cotton decided to leave England quickly because the

Reverend John Cotton preached about the Covenant of Grace, an idea that Anne herself came to believe in deeply.

authorities were after him. In 1633 he sailed to America on a boat called the *Griffin,* hoping he would find people who would support him and share his belief in the Covenant of Grace.

Several years earlier, in 1619, the Pilgrims had been the first group actually to break away from the Church. They had left England with one desire—to build a community where people could worship freely. They wanted to worship without having to obey rules or being questioned by the Church of England. The **Massachusetts Bay Colony** was built for one purpose—to provide a place of religious freedom for Puritans.

Just as the English government had been a theocracy, the Massachusetts Bay Colony would be ruled politically by the religious rulers. Instead of being governed by the strict Church of England, the new colony would be under Puritan control. One of the men who most wanted to establish the Massachusetts Bay Colony was John Winthrop. He planned to build a city that would show the Church of England what England could become if only they would allow the Puritans to govern and to worship freely. The all-Puritan Massachusetts Bay Colony was exactly where John Cotton and his wife chose to make their new home.

When John Cotton left England, Anne Hutchinson lost her teacher. Soon afterward, two of her daughters died, leaving Anne with much sadness and many questions. She studied the Bible and prayed, and she kept thinking about a person's individual relationship with God. She became even more convinced that the Covenant of Grace was true–that God's love was more important than good works. She could not stand to live in England any longer without religious freedom and without the teaching she needed– the kind John Cotton had given her. She could see that life was not going to get easier for the Puritans in England anytime soon. Most people felt that the persecution would end sometime, but Anne was ready to leave immediately.

To escape persecution, many Puritans left England for the Massachusetts Bay Colony. This is how an artist imagined the colony celebrating the first Thanksgiving.

After Cotton went to America, Anne was wondering what to do one day and began to read her Bible. In the Book of Isaiah, chapter 30, verse 20, she read, "And though the Lord give you the bread of adversity, and the water of affliction, yet shall not thy teachers be removed into a corner any more, but thine eyes shall see thy teachers." Anne decided that she would indeed see John Cotton and listen to his sermons again. One year after Cotton left England, Anne and William Hutchinson and 11 of their children climbed aboard the same ship Reverend Cotton had sailed and headed for Massachusetts.

Many, many ships crossed the ocean in the 1600s, to explore and to settle new colonies. In 1634 Anne Hutchinson and her family sailed to America to start a new life, hoping to find the freedom of religion they were denied in England.

Speaking Her Mind

The *Griffin* was filled with passengers who were crossing the Atlantic Ocean and moving to America. Most wanted religious freedom, while others wanted the challenge and adventure of life in an unsettled land. The voyage from England to America took about two months and the first few weeks were not easy. The *Griffin* tossed upon the choppy waters and went through several storms, causing many passengers to become seasick. After the waters calmed, the travelers felt better. The boat was not comfortable, but they did find ways to survive the trip.

Each day a minister would preach a sermon in the bottom part of the boat. The Hutchinson family attended sermons daily, but Anne did not like the preaching of one of the ministers. Reverend Zechariah Symmes was known for being proud and for preaching sermons that sometimes lasted up to five hours. He also preached the Covenant of Works, which Anne was trying so hard to escape.

One day Reverend Symmes was preaching that certain qualities of life on earth—helping people, going to church often, or being successful in a job—would get people into heaven when they died. Anne Hutchinson disagreed. She believed that *anyone* could do good things and that good works did not earn people a place in heaven. She believed that it was possible for people to know inside themselves—in their hearts—that they would be saved from hell and that God loved them. She believed God could, and would, speak privately

Sailors at sea would often catch fish and keep them in large tubs of water on the deck of the ship until it was time to cook and eat the fish. The children on the *Griffin* often amused themselves by watching the fish swimming around in the tubs.

to people and assure them of salvation—if they would listen. Finally, she had heard enough of Symmes's sermon and walked out of the service before he had finished preaching.

When Symmes did finish his sermon, several women found Anne on the ship's upper deck. They knew she had been unhappy with Reverend Symmes's message and they wanted to know why. Several times before, both in England and on the ship, Mrs. Hutchinson had spoken to groups of women and explained sermons to them. Now she was telling them why she did not agree with Reverend Symmes.

But the women were not the only ones who wanted to talk to Anne. Zechariah Symmes was also curious about why she had left the meeting during his sermon. He found her, and asked if she had left because she did not feel well. She stood up to him and told him honestly how she felt about his teaching. She asked Reverend Symmes several questions, which he had trouble answering.

In those days, only ministers were allowed to explain the meaning of the Bible. Men rarely challenged them face-to-face, but women *never* challenged them. Reverend Symmes could tell that Anne Hutchinson was not a typical silent, frightened woman. He hoped he would not have to put up with her for long. He would find out soon enough.

Another event that called attention to Anne was that she told them that she felt the *Griffin* would reach New England on September 18, 1634, which is exactly when they landed. Because of this prediction and her disagreement with Zechariah Symmes, the other women knew Anne was strong and full of courage. Before she ever set foot on the soil of her new country, it was clear that Anne Hutchinson was different. In fact, after the boat landed, some of the ministers who had sailed on the *Griffin* warned other church leaders that Anne could cause trouble.

Unlike some of the other passengers on the

Griffin, Anne and William Hutchinson had a home to go to as soon as they landed. They had sent their son Edward ahead of them to New England, and the young man built a house that would be ready when the rest of the family arrived. After her experience with Zechariah Symmes, Anne must have been eager to settle into her new log cabin and her new community. But she must also have wondered how much religious freedom she would really have in Boston.

The minister of the church in Boston, Reverend John Wilson, did not preach the Covenant of Grace. But John Cotton was the church's teacher and Anne was eager to hear his preaching again, so she and William planned to join the church. Most of the time husbands and wives applied for membership together and were able to join the church at the same time.

One of Anne Hutchinson's first disappointments came when William was invited to join the church and she was not. In those days, people had to answer questions about their beliefs before they were admitted into the church. In October 1634 William received a letter from the church. They had approved his application immediately. Anne did not receive anything. She knew that any member of the church could object to a membership application and ask for the applicant to be investigated. Anne discovered that her troubles with Zechariah Symmes had not ended on the *Griffin.* He was the one who objected to her application.

M en used to be called either "Mister" or "Goodman," depending on their importance. The wife of a common, or less wealthy, man would be called "Goodwife" instead of "Mistress." But Anne Hutchinson was called "Mistress Hutchinson" because her husband was a successful cloth merchant and one of the colony's leading citizens.

She was asked to meet with some leaders to answer more questions about her beliefs. The men who questioned her were Governor Thomas Dudley, Reverend John Cotton, and Reverend Zechariah Symmes. They asked her what she believed, and she told them the truth.

In order to be accepted into the church, she did admit that she had been mistaken in some of her thinking. Privately she told herself that she surely had been wrong in certain matters, just not in her religion. She never admitted to being mistaken about religion, only to being mistaken in general, which seemed fair to her.

In spite of her earlier argument with Zechariah Symmes, the three men finally allowed her to join William as a member of the church. In those days men often believed that they were smarter than women and that women were too emotional. The men who questioned Anne Hutchinson thought that she would settle down and stop criticizing the Covenant of Works once she moved into a new house and concentrated on being a wife and a mother.

Anne did indeed get busy. The Hutchinsons moved into a roomy two-story house right across from the governor, in the best part of town. William had a successful business as a textile merchant, and Anne made sure that the cooking, cleaning, and laundry were done for her very large family. (Altogether William and Anne had 15 children, most of whom grew to adulthood.) In addition to all the work of caring for her own family, Anne delivered babies, made medicines, and helped take care of sick people. She also planted and maintained an herb garden and an orchard.

Anne discovered that the Puritan church in New England was, in its own way, just as strict as the Church of England. Many people, especially Anne Hutchinson, were disappointed because they were not enjoying the religious freedom they had expected in the new country. Even John Cotton warned her to be careful and not to speak much about her views and beliefs. The Puritans had left England because the Church of England would not allow

At the time Anne Hutchinson lived, homes did not have electricity. The people in the Massachusetts Bay Colony built fires in large stone fireplaces to heat their houses. For light, they made candles out of pine wood. These candles dripped tar, which became one of the most valuable items colonists could trade.

them freedom of worship. Now they would not allow others that freedom either. They believed that God wanted them to build a "pure" colony– a place where the Puritan faith would be the only faith allowed. They did not mind if other people settled around them, but they did everything they could to make sure only strict Puritans lived and worshipped in the Massachusetts Bay Colony. Anne Hutchinson knew that her life in the colony was going to be harder than she had thought.

Anne hosted weekly religious meetings in her home to discuss the minister's sermons and to express her own opinions on religion. Before long, dozens of people began attending, very interested in what she had to say.

The Troubles Begin

The Hutchinsons contributed to the colony in several ways. The men respected William and allowed him to be a magistrate—one of the city leaders. He was also a successful merchant who made enough money to build his family the largest house in the colony. Anne was known as a kind, generous, helpful woman and had a good reputation as a midwife and nurse.

Even though Anne had not been able to join the church immediately, she became quite popular after she did. John Cotton, for one, knew she was smart, and others began to realize that she understood more about God than most people did. In those days, small groups often gathered once a week for religious meetings in someone's home. The groups always started their meetings by discussing the sermon they had heard the previous Sunday.

Before long, Anne Hutchinson was hosting one of these meetings in her home. She would do her best to explain what John Cotton had preached that week. Then she would talk more about some of his beliefs, sometimes adding her own opinions to what he had said and saying more than what he really believed. Eventually, she even began to criticize some of the ministers, which was unacceptable to the leaders of the colony.

In the fall of 1636 John Winthrop began to think that Mrs. Hutchinson's beliefs could be dangerous to the colony. The number of people who visited her weekly meetings kept growing and growing. Only six women had come to her first meeting, but a week later 60 showed up. Then she added a second weekly

John Winthrop came to America in 1630 aboard the *Arabella* as the leader of the Massachusetts Bay Company. Under his direction as a 12-term governor of the Massachusetts Bay Colony, Boston was founded.

meeting for men. Winthrop could tell by their excited conversation and by the smiles on their faces as they left the Hutchinson house that they were devoted to Anne Hutchinson and that they agreed with her.

John Winthrop saw Anne Hutchinson as a threat to his dream of keeping the Massachusetts Bay Colony a purely Puritan community. Luckily for him, he was able to keep his eye on everyone who came and went from the Hutchinson home because he lived right across the street. He was thinking quickly and carefully about how to silence Anne Hutchinson and bring everyone back into agreement with his kind of Puritanism.

By the end of October 1636, those who supported Anne Hutchinson and the Covenant of Grace decided they needed someone to speak for them in the church. They began to look for a person who would be their official representative. Anne Hutchinson was the natural choice, but because she was a woman, no one would dare nominate her for a church office. Fortunately for them, she had a brother-in-law who was a minister and could represent them almost as well.

Reverend John Wheelwright was married to William Hutchinson's sister. He and his family had arrived in the colony in June 1634. He, too, believed and preached the Covenant of Grace and had moved to America after being in trouble with the authorities in England. Anne Hutchinson and those who agreed with her were happy that Wheelwright had come to Boston. In fact, they wanted him to become a teacher in the church and to work with John Cotton. That way, though they would still have to endure John Wilson's preaching about the Covenant of Works, they could also learn from John Cotton and John Wheelwright. But neither John Wilson nor John Winthrop would allow that to happen.

When the church held a meeting on October 30, 1636, someone requested that that the church vote to make John Wheelwright their second teacher. As more and more people moved into the colony, the church was growing and they wondered if it was now time to have three ministers instead of two. Immediately, John Winthrop said that there was no need for another minister and opposed Wheelwright's election as a teacher.

The church discussed the issue, with strong opinions coming from people on both sides. Eventually Winthrop was able to stop Wheelwright's election, but it was not an easy battle. In the end he had hurt the feelings of many people and even lost some of his friends. After Winthrop led the block against Wheelwright's election, many church members grew to dislike Winthrop and Wilson more and more. Although Wilson was still the pastor, John Cotton was the most popular minister. Winthrop had made people angry and Wilson did not have much respect from the members. Wilson and Winthrop blamed Anne Hutchinson for the trouble in the church. They knew they had to do something.

By the beginning of 1637, the Massachusetts Bay Colony was not at all the peaceful, perfect

HENRY VANE.

Like Anne, Governor Henry Vane believed in the Covenant of Grace. When Vane lost power, Anne lost a powerful supporter.

society John Winthrop wanted it to be. Instead, it was an angry place, full of arguing between those who supported Winthrop and Wilson and those who supported Anne Hutchinson and Henry Vane, the popular young governor who believed in the Covenant of Grace. On January 20, the **General Court** declared a fast—a time of going without food—for the purpose of getting everyone to think about the religious problems in the colony.

One afternoon during the fast, John Wheelwright showed up at a lecture being given by John Cotton. When Reverend Cotton had finished, Wheelwright spoke angrily against ministers who preached the Covenant of Works and made it clear that he thought many of the colony's rulers should not be in positions of leadership. Soon afterward, he was convicted of **sedition**—speaking against the government—for which he could be forced to leave the colony. His sentence would not be announced until the next meeting of the General Court, which would be held in May.

May was the month in which the colony elected new leaders. Two of the most important items for the court were deciding how to punish

Wheelwright and electing new officials. When the court gathered, they were given a letter signed by many people in the colony asking them not to punish Wheelwright. Governor Henry Vane wanted to take care of the situation with Wheelwright before any other business was done by the court, but Winthrop and the leaders refused to do anything before the election. Vane let them have their way and held the election. When it was over, he had lost his seat as governor to John Winthrop and, in fact, had not been elected to any position at all. This was not good news for Anne Hutchinson and her supporters.

Ann Hutcheson

At a time when most women had little education and were expected simply to stay home and raise children, Anne was strong-minded, intelligent, and very accomplished. In addition to her extensive religious work, she delivered babies, acted as a nurse, kept a garden and orchard, and took care of her own large family.

Mrs. Hutchinson on Trial

With Winthrop in the governor's seat, Henry Vane prepared to leave the colony and return to England. Anne Hutchinson would lose one of her biggest supporters and one of the people who made her life easier when he was the governor. She knew that she would have a harder time than ever with Winthrop in control.

She was right. On August 30, after Winthrop's election in May, all the ministers from the Massachusetts Bay Colony, including John Cotton and John Wheelwright, met with a group of ministers from nearby Connecticut. For almost four weeks they talked about the religious **doctrines**, or beliefs, that were upsetting the colony. At the end of the meeting, they had a list of 82 items that were not acceptable to the church. Only John Wheelwright disagreed with the list. John Cotton had a hard time deciding how to vote on the list, but in the end he voted for it. His support of the list would cause many people to rethink their beliefs.

The Puritans believed that people should wear very plain clothing. In 1634, the same year that Anne Huchinson arrived in America, the Massachusetts General Court passed laws against fancy clothes. They would not allow people to buy clothes with silver, gold, silk, or lace on them, and they would not let people wear ruffles, or hats made of beaver skin.

Beliefs that are not acceptable to the church are called heresies. This group of ministers decided that anyone who taught or believed any **heresy** on the list would be questioned and possibly punished. The list would force people to say what they really believed. Then those who were guilty of believing things that were on the list could be dealt with and John Winthrop could have the pure colony he wanted.

The General Court began by sending John Wheelwright away from the colony. They also punished everyone who had signed the letter asking that Wheelwright not be sentenced for sedition. Anne Hutchinson knew the court would not leave her alone, that sooner or later they would bring charges against her. After all, the list of 82 items did include questioning ministers in church and women holding meetings about religious beliefs. Anne had done both.

The list of 82 errors was given to the church members more for them to think about than for them to obey. Anne Hutchinson and her followers chose to ignore them. They continued to question preachers and to meet weekly at her home.

Even though most of Anne's beliefs were included on the list, she could not be punished for what she thought. She could only be punished for what she said or did. John Winthrop called her to appear before the court. He was determined to put an end to her teaching and to discover even the smallest action for which he could punish her.

Her trial was scheduled to begin one chilly November morning. With William beside her, Anne made her way cautiously to the **meeting house** in the village of Newtown. Even though people had to make a great effort to get to the trial, many were there. Some were just curious, while others were there to support Anne. In addition to Governor John Winthrop and John Cotton, there were several magistrates and ministers there to hear and judge the trial. Reverend Zechariah Symmes was sitting with the ministers. Thomas Dudley, who thought Anne had been led astray by the devil, was there. Reverend John Wilson, who had wanted to punish Mrs. Hutchinson for a long time, was among the judges. As Anne looked at the men who would try her case, she did not see many who liked her. In fact, she could only be certain that she had one friend—John Cotton.

Winthrop opened the trial by saying, "Mrs. Hutchinson, you are called here as one of those

Called to answer for beliefs that fell within the church leaders' long list of "heresies," Anne was put on trial in the hopes they could find some way to silence her teaching.

that have troubled the peace of the common-wealth and the churches here. You are known to be a woman that hath a great share in the promoting and divulging of those opinions that are causes of this trouble." In other words, he told her that she had caused a lot of trouble in the Massachusetts Bay Colony and upset the churches because she taught the Covenant of Grace.

Winthrop gave her the chance to apologize and bring herself into agreement with the teaching of the church. If she continued speaking her mind about religious matters, he told her, the court would find a way to keep her from bothering anyone in the future. She understood what he meant. She would be banished—forced to move away—from the colony forever.

What she did not hear was a specific charge against her. She looked at Winthrop and said, "I am called here to answer before you but I hear no things laid to my charge." In many ways Anne Hutchinson was smarter than John Winthrop. She was not afraid of him and quickly insisted that he name the charge against her. Winthrop told her that she was thought to be guilty of sedition, of holding meetings in her house after the ministers had discouraged them in August, of not supporting the ministers and the churches, and of supporting John Wheelwright. Finally, he told her, she had broken the fifth of the Ten Commandments, which says to honor your father and mother. "Father and mother" meant anyone who had authority, said Winthrop, including the founding fathers of the colony.

Anne argued with Winthrop on that point. He was frustrated because it was becoming obvious that she truly was smarter than he. In fact, she was a strong and brilliant woman. She was not afraid of Governor Winthrop or of the court. She would not make it easy for them to send her away from the colony.

Next the court asked her to defend the weekly meetings she had held in her home. She answered them by quoting two different

Accused at her trial of having "troubled the peace of the commonwealth and the churches," Anne demanded to know exactly what she was charged with. Among other things she was told she had insulted the ministers and was causing other colonists to question church leadership.

Scriptures. In one place, the Bible says for older women to instruct younger women. In the other place, it says that people who know a lot should teach those who do not know as much. Both Scriptures seemed to indicate that Anne Hutchinson's meetings should not have been a problem.

The court decided that the Scriptures did not give her the right to hold religious meetings in her home because she was not a minister. She disagreed and asked the court if her name needed to be written in the Bible for them to believe her meetings and her teaching were not a sin.

The court was angry that she had tried to use the Bible to support her. They told her that she was causing people to be unhappy with the church and to question the church leadership. They would not allow her to continue her meetings.

Finally they moved to the last accusation against her—that she had insulted the ministers of the church. Actually, the ministers had held a conference with her some months earlier. She had been urged to tell them exactly how she felt and what she believed. They promised her the meeting would be private.

Now some of the same men who were supposed to keep that meeting secret were telling everyone what she had said. The main point was that she had accused all the ministers, except John Cotton and John Wheelwright, of believing and preaching in the Covenant of Works. The ministers testified against her, but she did not believe they were telling the truth.

That night she looked at notes from the meeting. John Wilson, one of those who was most strongly against her, had taken the notes. Just as she thought, his notes did not match what the ministers had said in court. The next morning, she demanded that the ministers give their testimonies again—this time under oath. She had gotten the ministers into a difficult position. If they gave their testimony under oath and were found to be wrong, they would be guilty of lying in court and of taking the name of the Lord in vain. Both charges were very serious.

None of the ministers wanted to speak under oath. Finally, John Cotton spoke first. Even though other ministers pressured him, he told the court he did not believe Mrs. Hutchinson accused the ministers of preaching or believing in the Covenant of Works.

After he had spoken, it looked like Mrs. Hutchinson might win her case. The first two charges had not been strong enough to get her banished, though she would have been lectured. The third charge did not stand because of John Cotton's words. After two days of questioning and careful answers from Mrs. Hutchinson, she herself began to speak the words that turned the tide against her.

No one knows exactly why, but for some reason, Mrs. Hutchinson began to speak against the colony and tell them that God would curse them for bringing her to trial. At first, governor Winthrop tried to stop her. Then he may have

A Puritan summons worshipers to church by beating a drum. Although the Puritans first came to America to escape religious persecution, they themselves became intolerant of anyone who disagreed with their strict beliefs.

realized that she was about to get herself in trouble. As she continued, she told the court that God had revealed to her that she would be persecuted in America. The Puritans did not believe that God showed people the future. The court asked her if it might have been the devil and not God who had given her the revelation.

Anne believed that God had shown her what would happen, and told them that He had spoken to her "by the voice of his own spirit to my soul." With those words, she convicted herself of heresy. The Puritans did not believe God spoke personally to anyone, but that He spoke only through His ministers. The court believed that God would punish them if they allowed Anne Hutchinson to stay in the colony, knowing she was a heretic.

At last, the court found Anne guilty and Governor Winthrop punished her by forcing her from the colony.

A majestic statue of Anne and one of her children reminds the visitors to modern-day Massachusetts that not all the influential people of colonial times were men. Though women had virtually no power in those days, a few—like Anne Hutchinson—had a great impact on history.

Faithful to
the End

ecause she was expecting a baby and because
the winter was terribly cold and icy, Governor Winthrop did not make Anne Hutchinson leave
the colony immediately after her trial. Instead, she
was placed under **house arrest**—forced to stay at
home—for four months. She stayed in the town of
Roxbury, in the home of Joseph Welde, a friend
of Reverend Wilson. Only her family and the ministers were allowed to visit her. During this lonely time
Anne was able to spend much time reading the
Bible, praying, and thinking about her faith. When
ministers came to visit, she asked many questions
and spoke openly of her struggles. The ministers

could not answer all of her questions, but they did not forget them.

While she was under house arrest, many of her followers, called Hutchinsonians, were also questioned by the authorities. Some of them said that they no longer believed in the Covenant of Grace. Others had to appear before the court to be banished, fined, or lose their right to vote. One group even left the colony on their own.

When spring came, Anne had to be taken before the Boston church one more time before she was forced to leave the colony forever. The church leaders had decided that, even if she moved out of the Massachusetts Bay Colony, she would still be a part of the church unless they excommunicated her by declaring that she was no longer a member of the church. They needed to let her know that the church no longer accepted her.

On March 15, 1638, a crowd had gathered to hear Anne Hutchinson's sentence. When she arrived at the meeting house, she did not have much support, but people were shocked to see how old and tired she looked. She had struggled bravely as she fought for her beliefs, and her eyes had the sad, weary look of a defeated soldier.

Many of her friends had either left the colony or were afraid to be on her side anymore. Even her husband, William, was not present that day. He was so sure that Anne would be told to leave the colony that he had taken a team of 19 men to search for a place to build a new home outside the Massachusetts Bay Colony. Several of their adult sons had been with him, but Edward, the oldest, was able to travel back to Boston in time to be with his mother at the meeting. The only people she could count on in the audience were Edward and his wife, her daughter, Faith, and Faith's husband. Her loyal friend Mary Dyer was also there.

Her trouble was not finished. At the church, Anne discovered that the ministers who had visited her at Joseph Welde's house had brought

Anne's good friend Mary Dyer supported her during the difficult times and especially at her harsh sentencing by the church leaders. The fate of Mary herself turned out to be even worse: she was eventually executed for her religious beliefs.

more charges against her. She thought the ministers had come to help her, once the trial was over. Now they had betrayed her again. She spent nine long hours answering more questions and arguing with the ministers. As hard as that was, the hardest part was knowing that even John Cotton, the teacher she admired and followed for almost 20 years, had turned against her. Near the end of the day, the church had to vote on whether or not to admonish—publicly scold—Anne Hutchinson for her beliefs. In order to admonish her, everyone in the church had to vote in favor of it. Two people voted against it— her son, Edward, and her son-in-law, Thomas Savage. (In those days, women were not allowed to vote in the church.)

Some people did not like it that those two men from Anne's family were keeping her from being scolded in public. Someone suggested that Edward Hutchinson and Thomas Savage also be considered for admonishment, which meant they could not vote. Without those two votes, the church voted 100 percent to admonish Anne Hutchinson and the two young men. Perhaps worst of all, John Cotton was appointed to give the scolding

She stood before John Cotton, the one from whom she had learned so much, and listened as he gave the details of her errors. He spoke of the harm she had done to the church and of the danger that others could fall into if they agreed with her. She had given up everything to follow God; she believed with all her heart that what she spoke was true. Now she was accused of leading other people into sin and even of bringing dishonor to God.

When it seemed things could not get worse, Anne Hutchinson had to spend the next week in John Cotton's home. While she was there, she admitted that perhaps she had been wrong with her questions and doubts. The next Thursday, she went back to the meeting house and told everyone that, before she went to prison, she had not believed everything of which they now accused her. The ministers disagreed, saying that she had held her beliefs for years. Finally, John Cotton announced his decision that she must be forced to leave the colony and the church. Pastor Wilson excommunicated her, essentially saying that she was no longer a Christian and turning her over to the devil.

Anne Hutchinson's life in the New World had never been easy, but how could she have imagined it would end with **banishment** from the colony and **excommunication** from the church? Yet she was not the first person forced to leave. In 1636 the Puritans had banished a man named Roger Williams because he had different ideas than the authorities on many issues. He had founded Rhode Island, and now, in March 1638, the Hutchinsons were on their way to join him there.

They left the Massachusetts Bay Colony the day after Anne's sentence was pronounced. Anne's younger children had been staying with faithful friends, some of whom decided to leave the colony with the Hutchinsons. Edward got the family together, along with the food and clothing they could carry, and they started quickly on their journey. They knew that the leaders wanted them out of the colony immediately, and they did not want create any more trouble.

Traveling was terribly hard. Anne's baby would be born soon, so it was not easy for her to make a long journey on foot. There were no roads through the deep woods between Boston and Rhode Island, so they had no choice but to walk. Also, the warmth of spring had not come as they had expected and the weather was still cold and icy. It was so bad that the travelers stopped to spend a few days with some relatives who lived on a farm outside of Boston. They could not stay for long. The air was still chilly when they started again. For six days they trudged through the forest, sleeping at night on the hard, frozen ground. Just when Anne could not walk any further and almost collapsed, they arrived at Providence, the Rhode Island settlement Roger Williams had started.

William Hutchinson had chosen for his family to live on an island the Indians called Aquidneck, not more than a day's walk from Providence. By the time Anne reached the island, she was hardly strong enough to greet William. Several weeks later, she gave birth to her baby, but the child was stillborn. For a few days, the family wondered if Anne would die too. For months she was too sick even to get out of bed.

Eventually she did get well and regained her strength. The people on Aquidneck Island did not build a church, but held prayer meetings in one another's houses. Anne did not preach or teach as she had done before, but she did enjoy the small gatherings with her friends and finally felt free to worship as she desired. After a few years Anne was settled in her new community, happy and healthy. She was looking forward to growing old peacefully on the island. But in the spring of 1642, William Hutchinson became ill and died.

After his death, Anne moved with her six youngest children to a Dutch settlement in New York. In those days, settlers had to watch out for Indians, who might attack or rob them. Anne was not afraid of the Indians and even made friends with some of them when she lived on Aquidneck Island. Her sons warned her often to be careful around the Indians in New York, but Anne believed it was possible to live peacefully with them if the white people treated them fairly.

In 1643, Anne and all but one of her children living with her were killed when Indians raided their settlement. The people had been told that the Indians were angry and could attack. Some families hid in a Dutch fort and were not hurt. Anne, her family, and a few other families stayed and suffered violent deaths in the attack. Only one daughter, little Susanna, survived and was captured by the

Some colonists and Indians got along, but others were hostile toward each other. This Puritan family is defending itself from an Indian attack.

Indians. She had never been afraid of Indians and had, in fact, befriended an Indian brave. This man pitied her and adopted her as his own daughter. She was later rescued, but she did not

Even though Anne befriended some of the Indians who lived near her family in New York, they fell victims to a raid by the Indians in 1643.

want to go back to live among the English people.

Anne Hutchinson was a woman of courage and determination. The Puritan leaders in the Massachusetts Bay Colony believed that her murder by the Indians proved that God did not approve of her beliefs. Anne, on the other hand, had spent her life in prayer and Bible reading. She had truly tried to love God with all of her heart. She was not afraid to speak exactly what she believed, knowing that her opinions would not be popular with the leaders of her city. More than any other colonial woman, she paved the way for religious freedom in America.

Today many people do believe exactly as Anne Hutchinson did–that God does speak to people individually and that no amount of good works will assure a person's salvation. She believed to the end, and fought courageously for the Covenant of Grace and for grace alone.

GLOSSARY

banishment being forced to move out of a particular city or country

Covenant of Grace the belief that people are saved by god's love and not by good deeds

Covenant of Works the belief that good works earn salvation

doctrine beliefs of a certain group

excommunication being forced to leave a church

General Court the ministers and leaders who served as judges in the Massachusetts Bay Colony

heresy teachings that go against the beliefs of a certain religion

house arrest having to stay in a house and keep certain rules, instead of in a prison

Massachusetts Bay Colony the colony near present-day Boston that was founded as a place where people would have religious freedom and be governed by Puritan leaders

meeting house the place where church services and other colonial activities were held

Puritans people who left the Church of England because they felt it was too much like the Catholic Church

sedition rebelling against the government

theocracy a government in which the church and the state rule together

CHRONOLOGY

1591 Anne Marbury is born in Alford, England.

1612 Anne marries William Hutchinson.

1629 English Puritans decide to leave England to set up their own city in America.

1633 Reverend John Cotton, Anne Hutchinson's teacher, sails to America.

1634 Anne and William Hutchinson and most of their children arrive in America; Anne and William are allowed to be members of the church at Boston.

1635 Henry Vane arrives in America; he is admitted to the Boston church.

1636 Henry Vane, a supporter of Anne Hutchinson, is elected governor of Massachusetts; John Winthrop regains the governor's seat the next year.

1637 John Wheelwright is found guilty of sedition; Anne Hutchinson is brought to trial.

1638 Anne is found guilty of heresy and forced to leave the colony; the Hutchinsons join Roger Williams's colony in Rhode Island.

CHRONOLOGY

1642 Anne's husband, William, dies.

1643 Anne Hutchinson and all but one of her children are killed by Indians.

COLONIAL TIME LINE

1607 Jamestown, Virginia, is settled by the English.

1620 Pilgrims on the *Mayflower* land at Plymouth, Massachusetts.

1623 The Dutch settle New Netherland, the colony that later becomes New York.

1630 Massachusetts Bay Colony is started.

1634 Maryland is settled as a Roman Catholic colony. Later Maryland becomes a safe place for people with different religious beliefs.

1636 Roger Williams is thrown out of the Massachusetts Bay Colony. He settles Rhode Island, the first colony to give people freedom of religion.

1682 William Penn forms the colony of Pennsylvania.

1688 Pennsylvania Quakers make the first formal protest against slavery.

1692 Trials for witchcraft are held in Salem, Massachusetts.

1712 Slaves revolt in New York. Twenty-one blacks are killed as punishment.

COLONIAL TIME LINE

1720 Major smallpox outbreak occurs in Boston. Cotton Mather and some doctors try a new treatment. Many people think the new treatment shouldn't be used.

1754 French and Indian War begins. It ends nine years later.

1761 Benjamin Banneker builds a wooden clock that keeps precise time.

1765 Britain passes the Stamp Act. Violent protests break out in the colonies. The Stamp Act is ended the next year.

1775 The battles of Lexington and Concord begin the American Revolution.

1776 Declaration of Independence is signed.

FURTHER READING

Fradin, Dennis Brindell. *Anne Hutchinson: Fighter for Religious Freedom*. Hillside, N.J.: Enslow Publishers, 1990.

——. *The Massachusetts Colony*. Chicago: Children's Press, 1987.

IlgenFritz, Elizabeth. *Anne Hutchinson*. New York: Chelsea House Publishers, 1991.

Nichols, Joan Kane. *A Matter of Conscience: The Trial of Anne Hutchinson*. Austin, Tex.: Steck-Vaughn Publishers, 1993.

Wayne, Bennett, Ed. *Women with a Cause*. Champaign, Ill.: Garrard Publishing Co., 1975.

INDEX

Catholic Church, 7–8
Charles I, King, 14
Church of England
  establishment of, 7–8
  Hutchinson's father opposed to, 8,
    10, 11
  Pilgrims breaking away from, 16
  Puritans opposed to, 8, 10, 14, 16
  Puritans persecuted by, 10, 14, 16, 17
  and woman ministers, 11, 12
Cotton, Reverend John
  arrest of, 14
  and Covenant of Grace, 13–14, 16
  and Covenant of Works, 13, 14
  and move to Massachusetts Bay
    Colony, 14, 16, 17
  and Puritans, 12–16
  and religious freedom, 28
  and Wheelwright, 35, 38
Covenant of Grace, 13–14, 16, 34, 35,
  36, 46, 56, 67
Covenant of Works, 13, 14, 22, 25, 27,
  35, 38

Dudley, Thomas, 26, 44
Dyer, Mary, 57

Freedom of religion. *See* Religious
  freedom

General Court, 41–53
Griffin, 16, 21–25

Henry VIII, King, 7–8
Heresy(ies)
  Hutchinson found guilty of, 41–53
  list of, 41–43
Hutchinson, Anne
  and banishment from colony, 53,
    55–61

birth of, 7
childhood of, 7, 10–11
children of, 12, 17, 19, 25, 28, 57, 59,
  61–62, 64–66
and Church of England, 12, 13
and Cotton, 17, 25, 26, 28, 31, 44,
  51, 59, 60, 61
and Covenant of Grace, 13, 14, 17,
  34, 46, 56, 67
and Covenant of Works, 13, 14, 22,
  27, 50, 51
education of, 11
excommunication of, 56, 61
family of, 7, 8–11
father of, 7, 8, 10–11
husband of, 12, 19, 25–26, 27, 28,
  31, 44, 57, 63, 64
murder of, 64, 66–67
and religious freedom, 17, 25, 28–
  29, 34, 67
trial of, 41–53
and weekly religious meetings, 32,
  34, 43, 47, 49
Hutchinson, Edward (son), 25, 57,
  59–60, 62
Hutchinson, Susanna (daughter), 64–
  66
Hutchinson, William (husband), 12, 19,
  25–26, 27, 28, 31, 44, 57, 63, 64
Hutchinsonians, 56

Marbury, Bridget (mother), 7
Marbury, Reverend Francis (father),
  7, 8, 10–11
Massachusetts Bay Colony
  Cotton's move to, 16, 17
  Hutchinson's move to, 17–19, 21–25
  Puritans in, 16–17, 25, 28–29
  and religious freedom, 16, 17, 25,
    28–29, 32, 34

INDEX

Native Americans, 64, 66–67
New York, Hutchinson's move to, 64

Pilgrims, 16
Puritans
  beliefs of, 8
  Church of England opposed by, 8,
    10, 14, 16
  and Covenant of Grace, 13–14, 16
  in Massachusetts Bay Colony, 16–17,
    25, 28–29
  persecution of by Church of Eng-
    land, 10, 14, 16, 17
  and religious freedom, 16–17, 25,
    28–29

Religious freedom
  and Cotton, 28
  and England, 10, 11, 14, 16, 17, 28–
    29
  and Hutchinson, 17, 25, 28–29, 34, 67
  and Massachusetts Bay Colony, 16,
    17, 25, 28–29, 32, 34
Rhode Island
  Hutchinson's move to, 61–64
  Williams as founder of, 61, 63

Savage, Thomas (son-in-law), 59–60
Symmes, Reverend Zechariah, 22–24,
    25, 26, 27, 44

Vane, Henry, 38–39, 41

Welde, Joseph, 55, 57
Wheelwright, Reverend John, 47, 50
  as guilty of sedition, 38–39, 41, 43
  and list of heresies, 41, 42
  as teacher, 35–36
Williams, Roger, 61, 63
Wilson, Reverend John, 25, 35, 36,
    37, 44, 50
Winthrop, John
  and establishment of Massachusetts
    Bay Colony, 16–17
  as governor, 39, 41
  and Hutchinson, 32, 34, 35–37, 41,
    43–44, 46–47, 51, 53, 55
  and list of heresies, 42
  and Wheelwright, 35–36

PICTURE CREDITS

ABOUT THE AUTHORS ═══════

BETH CLARK works in the Christian publishing industry in Nashville, Tennessee. A graduate of the Hutchinson School and Centre College, she has an active interest in reading, writing, and the history of religion and revival.

Senior Consulting Editor **ARTHUR M. SCHLESINGER, JR.** is the leading American historian of our time. He won the Pulitzer Prize for his book *The Age of Jackson* (1945) and again for *A Thousand Days* (1965). This chronicle of the Kennedy Administration also won a National Book Award. He has written many other books including a multi-volume series, *The Age of Roosevelt*. Professor Schlesinger is the Albert Schweitzer Professor of the Humanities at the City University of New York, and has been involved in several other Chelsea House projects, including the REVOLUTIONARY WAR LEADERS biographies on the most prominent figures of early American history.